ADVENTURES OF SOL
A JOURNEY TO SELF-LOVE

Written and Illustrated by
Jennie Blackwood and Alyssa Blackwood

Balboa Press books may be ordered through booksellers or by contacting:

Balboa Press
A Division of Hay House
1663 Liberty Drive
Bloomington, IN 47403
www.balboapress.com
844-682-1282

ISBN: 979-8-7652-5115-7 (sc)
ISBN: 979-8-7652-5116-4 (hc)
ISBN: 979-8-7652-5114-0 (e)

Library of Congress Control Number: 2024909646

Print information available on the last page.

Balboa Press rev. date: 06/26/2024

BALBOA.PRESS
A DIVISION OF HAY HOUSE

ADVENTURES OF SOL
A JOURNEY TO SELF-LOVE

Hi, I'm Sol!
Come along with me
on our journey
to self-love!

I have a strong mind.
I have a strong body.
I am a strong soul.

I am love.
I give and receive love.
I am surrounded by love.

I am positive.
I have a positive mind.
I am surrounded by positive energy.

I am kind.
I am kind to others.
Others are kind to me.
I am kind to myself.

I am honest.
I am honest with others.
Others are honest with me.
I am honest with myself.

I am helpful.
I help others.
Others help me.
I speak up when I need help.
I help myself.

I am a good friend.
I attract good people in my life.
Good things happen for me.
I am good to myself.

I am a good listener.
I listen to others.
Others listen to me.
I listen to my heart.

9

I am caring.
I care about others.
Others care about me.
I care about myself.

I smile a lot.
I smile at others.
Others smile at me.
I smile at myself.

I am grateful.
I am grateful for my family.
I am grateful for my friends.
I am grateful for myself.

I am limitless.
I can do anything.
I believe in myself.

I am and do my best.
I help others be and do their best.
I am my best self.

I am confident.
I help others feel confident.
I am confident in my decisions.
I am confident in myself.

I forgive.
I forgive others.
Others forgive me.
I forgive myself.

It's OK to make mistakes.

I learn and grow from my mistakes,
and I apply them to my decisions.

I make good decisions.

I am respectful.
I respect others.
Others respect me.
I respect myself.

I am loyal.
I am loyal to my family and friends.
My family and friends are loyal to me.
I am loyal to myself.

I am creative.
I create from my heart.
My heart creates with me.

I create my own happiness.
Happy thoughts create happy feelings.
Happy feelings help me create
from my heart.

I am peace.

I am love.

I am joy.

23

Thank you for coming on this journey with me to self-love! I will see you soon on our next adventure!

Pick your favorite affirmations and feel-good words. Write them on a sticky note and put them on your mirror and/or all over your house. Have your parent, grandparent, sister, brother, and/or any loved one do the same, and share the love and positivity it will bring to all your lives. You can also have fun creating your own affirmations and feel-good words together!

Positive Affirmations and Feel-Good Words From Soul!

I have a strong mind.

I have a strong body.

I am a strong soul.

I am love.

I am positive.

I am kind.

I am honest.

I am helpful.

I am a good friend.

I am a good listener.

I smile a lot.

I am caring.

I am respectful.

I am loyal.

I am grateful.

I am limitless.

I am and do my best.

I am confident.

I am patient.

I make good decisions.

I forgive.

I am creative.

I create my own happiness.

I am peace.

I am amazing the way I am.

I am joy.

I am smart.

I have fun.

Everything works out for me.

I am healthy.

I am compassionate.

I am brave.

I love to laugh.

I am happy.

Jennie, a caring mother of 2 and college graduate, and her niece Alyssa, specializing in digital art design, both from California, team up to present a children's book that is light hearted and spreads the message of love. Both authors embrace their own everyday world with passion, love and positive thinking. Their vibrant smiles bring peace, love and joy to the people around them. Together they want to share this with others in hopes that more people and children will live by those values as well as embrace their beautiful souls within.

Printed in the United States
by Baker & Taylor Publisher Services